Yates, Irene
All about shape

All About

SHAPE

All About
SHAPE

by Irene Yates
Illustrated by Jill Newton

BENCHMARK BOOKS

MARSHALL CAVENDISH
NEW YORK

Library of Congress Cataloging-in-Publication Data

Yates, Irene.
    All about shape / by Irene Yates ; illustrated by Jill Newton.
  p. cm.
    Summary: Describes a variety of shapes, including circles,
spheres, squares, rectangles, cubes, triangles, and others.
  ISBN 0-7614-0515-1 (lib. bdg.)
    1. Geometry—Juvenile literature. [1. Shape.] I. Newton, Jill,
date, ill. II. Title.
QA445.5.Y38 1998
516'.15—dc21   97-3963
                                                                    CIP
                                                                    AC

Benchmark Books
Marshall Cavendish Corporation
99 White Plains Road
Tarrytown, New York 10591

First published in Great Britain in 1997 by Belitha Press
Copyright in this format © Belitha Press 1997
Text copyright © Irene Yates 1997
Illustrations copyright © Jill Newton 1997
American edition © Marshall Cavendish Corporation 1998

Printed in Hong Kong

1 3 5 6 4 2

Contents

What is shape?

Shape is all around us. There are lots of different shapes. Some shapes have names. Which shape do you like best?

This is a shape wheel. You can see six different shapes here. Count the edges on each shape.

Everything in the world
has a shape. Sometimes
lots of different small
shapes make up
one large shape.

Here are some more
shapes. Do you know
what they are?

More about shape

There are two kinds of shapes. Some are flat, such as shapes drawn on paper, and some are not.

Shapes that are not flat are called solid shapes. You can pick them up and hold them.

This square is a flat shape with four edges and one side.

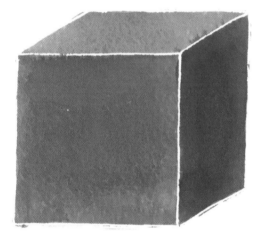

This cube is a solid shape. It has six sides. Each side has four edges.

Look at this shape. How many edges can you count? How many sides can you see?

Circles

Circles are round, flat shapes. If something is flat and almost round we call it a circular shape.

How many circular shapes can you see here? Can you name all the circular things on these pages?

The teeth on these wheels are called cogs. As they move, they fit together and push each other round.

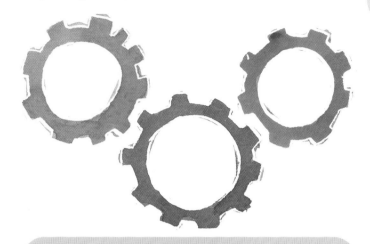

The rings inside a tree tell you how old it is.

Make a pattern

Draw a circle. Draw another circle so that they overlap. Draw lots more overlapping circles. Color in the spaces to make a pattern.

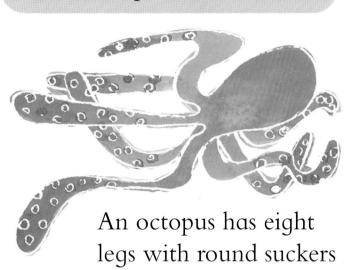

An octopus has eight legs with round suckers on each one.

Spheres

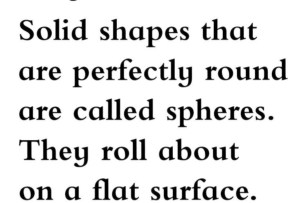

Solid shapes that
are perfectly round
are called spheres.
They roll about
on a flat surface.

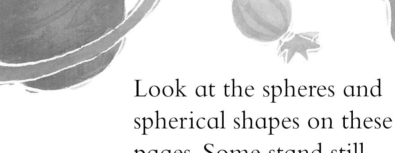

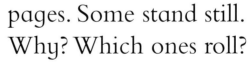

Look at the spheres and
spherical shapes on these
pages. Some stand still.
Why? Which ones roll?

Make a race track
Find some spheres and a thick card. Tilt the card and roll the spheres down it. Which rolls the fastest? Try tilting the card higher.

A sphere is a good shape to catch, throw and bounce.

An orange is a sphere. A wedge taken out of a sphere is called a segment.

A football looks like a sphere that has been stretched.

Cylinders

Cylinders are solid shapes with a circle at each end. The circles are the same size.

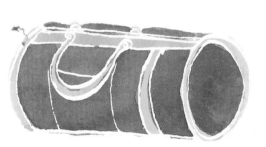

Look at all the cylinders here. What happens when you try to stack cylinders? Do they roll or do they stand still?

A wheel looks like a circle, but it is really a cylinder. It has a curved side joining the ends.

A **cylindrical** walk

Go for a cylindrical walk. Look for ten things that are cylinders or cylindrical shapes. What are they?

Bamboo grows in hot countries. Bamboo stems are cylinders.

The fingers on a glove are cylindrical shapes.

Squares and rectangles

Squares and rectangles are flat shapes with four corners and four straight edges.

Look at the squares and rectangles on these pages. What is the same about them? What is different?

The edges of a square measure the same. How many squares can you see in this square window?

The opposite edges of a rectangle measure the same. How many rectangles are there on this envelope?

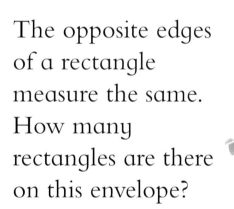

Make a rectangle

Draw six squares the same. Cut out the squares and paint them six colors. Fit them together to make different rectangles.

Cubes and cuboids

Cubes and cuboids are solid shapes. Their sides are squares and rectangles.

Cubes and cuboids are good shapes for containers because they hold a lot. Do you think they would stack easily?

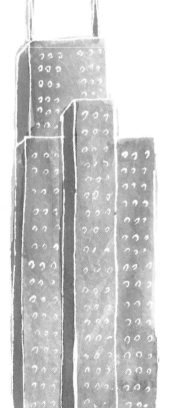

A cube has six square sides that all measure the same. These dice are cubes.

 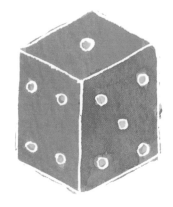

A cuboid has six sides. The opposite sides of a cuboid measure the same. These toy building blocks are cuboids.

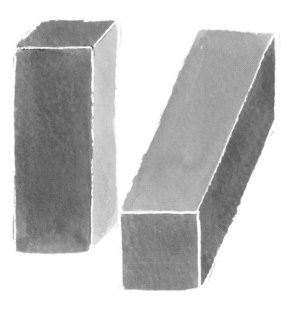

Make a box

Find a cube-shaped box. Carefully take it apart and make it into a flat shape. Now try to make it into a box again.

Food and drinks often come in cuboid-shaped boxes.

Triangles

Triangles are flat shapes. They have three sides and three corners.

Some shapes are almost triangles. There are lots of triangular shapes hidden on these pages. How many can you see?

Look for the
triangular shapes
on this Stegosaurus.

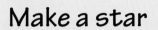

You can
find triangular
shapes in the leaves
and petals of plants.

Make a star
Draw two triangles.
Cut them out and put
one upside down on top
of the other to make a
star. Make lots of stars.

Some countries
have stamps that
are triangular.

More solid shapes

There are lots of solid shapes that have triangular sides.

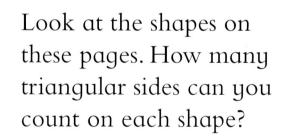

Look at the shapes on these pages. How many triangular sides can you count on each shape?

This pyramid has a square at the bottom. All the sides are triangles. The most famous pyramids are in Egypt.

Cones are a bit like curved pyramids. There is always a circle at the bottom. This wizard's hat is a cone.

Make a wizard's hat

Cut a circle out of paper. Cut from the edge of the circle to the center. Roll the paper into a cone and fix it with tape. Decorate it with stars.

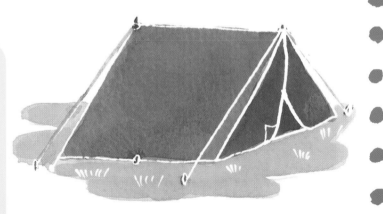

This tent has a triangle at each end and a rectangle for each side.

Regular shapes

When a shape has sides and corners that are all the same, it is called a regular shape.

Some of the shapes on this page are regular shapes. Can you see which ones they are?

Honeycombs are made up of shapes called hexagons. Are these regular hexagons?

This is a regular pentagon. It has five sides all the same. Is the bar of soap below a regular shape?

Make a collection

Make a collection of flat and solid regular shapes. Look for big and small things. Use a ruler to help you draw them.

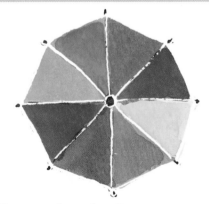

If you look down on an open umbrella, you can see it is a regular shape.

Other shapes

Some shapes don't have a name. They are called irregular shapes.

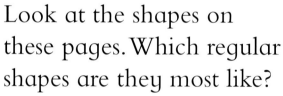

Look at the shapes on these pages. Which regular shapes are they most like?

Make an irregular shape
Use modeling clay to mold an unusual shape. Leave it to dry and harden. Paint your shape. Give it a name.

Clouds can be lots of different shapes.

A key is a special shape to fit into a key hole. It is an irregular shape.

A trumpet is a long tube with a wide end. Its shape helps it make a loud noise.

Explore shape

Make a tangram

1 Take a square piece of cardboard.
2 Draw lines on it exactly like these and color the shapes.
3 Cut along the lines.
4 Fit the pieces together to see how many different pictures you can make.

Make a net

Draw this shape on a piece of cardboard. Cut round the outside edge. Fold along all the other lines to build a pyramid.

Shape game

Have a competition with
a friend. See who can be first
to spot regular shapes at
school, in your home and
in the street. Make lists
and compare them.

Picture list

Here is a list of the pictures in this book.

Circles Tomato, tambourine, buttons, daisies, alarm clock, spectacles, pizza, cogs, tree trunk, cucumber slices, octopus.

Spheres Ice-cream balls, planet, candies, teapot, goldfish bowl, marbles, cherries, football, basketball, tennis ball, oranges, beads, football.

Cylinders Sausages, sports bag, candle, pencils and holder, Swiss roll, toy tanker, baked-bean can, wheel, bamboo, hose, gloves.

Squares and rectangles
Comic, photo in frame, checkered flag, xylophone, crackers, window and panes, kite, stamps on envelope, playing cards.

Cubes and cuboids Wrapped present, ice cubes, personal stereo, skyscraper, fish sticks and French fries, briefcase, dice, building blocks, food and drink boxes.

Triangles Mobile, piece of cheese, envelope, toy sailing boat, sandwich, shark fin, triangle, Stegosaurus, ivy leaves, lemon and orange slices, triangular stamp.

More solid shapes Ice-cream cone, seesaw, crayon, table lamp, mountaintops, house roof, pyramid, wizard's hat, tent.

Regular shapes Kite, octagon, tissue box, ring with cut stone, rubber, chocolate box, honeycomb, pentagon, bar of soap, umbrella.

Other shapes Pineapple, cutlery, shell, clothes peg, toy car, sneakers, clouds, key, trumpet, jelly.

Words to remember

circle a flat round shape.

cube a solid shape with square sides.

cuboid a solid shape with rectangular sides.

cylinder a solid curved shape with equal circles at each end.

rectangle a flat shape. Its corners are all the same but only its opposite sides are the same.

regular any shape with edges or sides that are all the same, and with corners that are all the same.

solid any shape that is not flat.

sphere a solid round shape.

square a flat shape. Its corners and its edges are all the same.

triangle a flat shape with three edges and three corners.